Giants on the Road

Armored Trucks

Norman D. Graubart

PowerKiDS press™

New York

Published in 2015 by The Rosen Publishing Group, Inc.
29 East 21st Street, New York, NY 10010

First Edition

Editor: Katie Kawa
Book Design: Jonathan J. D'Rozario

Photo Credits: Cover Siri Stafford/Photodisc/Getty Images; p. 5 Stephen Coburn/Shutterstock.com; pp. 6, 14, 22 ATABOY/The Image Bank/Getty Images; p. 9 Robert Alexander/Archive Photos/Getty Images; p. 10 (main) Fotocrisis/Shutterstock.com; p. 10 (inset) Africa Studio/Shutterstock.com; p. 13 Paul Conrath/ Digital Vision/Getty Images; p. 17 dade72/Shutterstock.com; p. 18 gueritos/iStock/Thinkstock.com; p. 21 Siri Stafford/Stone/Getty Images.

Library of Congress Cataloging-in-Publication Data

Graubart, Norman D.
Armored trucks / by Norman D. Graubart.
p. cm. — (Giants on the road)
Includes index.
ISBN 978-1-4994-0040-3 (pbk.)
ISBN 978-1-4994-0041-0 (6-pack)
ISBN 978-1-4994-0039-7 (library binding)
1. Trucks — Juvenile literature. I. Graubart, Norman D. II. Title.
TL230.15 G736 2015
629.224—d23

Manufactured in the United States of America

CPSIA Compliance Information: Batch #CW15PK: For Further Information contact Rosen Publishing, New York, New York at 1-800-237-9932

Contents

Have you ever seen an armored truck? They are giant!

5

"Armored" means "covered with a strong shell." That makes these trucks very safe.

Banks use armored trucks
to move money.

SECURITY SINCE
1859

26

DALLAS, TX
USDOT 076054
CA 1759
GVW 25,999

Sometimes armored trucks carry **jewelry**.

Armored truck drivers stay in the truck when items are moved in and out.

13

Guards ride in the trucks, too. They keep the things inside safe.

Only the driver and guards can get inside an armored truck!

18

England was the first country to use armored trucks.

Today, armored trucks are
all over the world.

21

Do you want to drive
an armored truck someday?

Words to Know

guards

jewelry

Index

Websites

Due to the changing nature of Internet links, PowerKids Press has developed an online list of websites related to the subject of this book. This site is updated regularly. Please use this link to access the list: www.powerkidslinks.com/gotr/atr